The Gospel of One

The Metaphysics of Revolution

By Mark Burke

DISCLAIMER

The content of The Gospel of One is for informational purposes only. Persons who need medical or psychological care should seek help from the appropriate health care professionals.

The Gospel of One:
The Metaphysics of Revolution

ISBN: 978-0-9831359-9-9

Dedication

This book is dedicated to the generations that follow and to all those who strive to make the Earth the best possible place it can be.

I, composed of nothing
Shape the stars
Beneath my feet

The Gospel of One

The Metaphysics of Revolution

Mark Burke

Descend now to the world of flesh
And for a time become Man.

Preface

Hello, and welcome to "The Gospel of One." This work is inspired by the higher ideas I read in the canonical gospels as a youth, and by a lifetime of experience acquired since.

As a young child, I sang, "Yes, Jesus loves me" in Sunday school classes and then went into the main chapel to hear the pastor declare that everyone falls short of God's expectations and all of us were going to burn in hell forever. Somehow, "Jesus loves me" didn't make it into the pastor's "fire and brimstone" sermons that always seemed to focus on guilt and punishment.

This created an image of God as an angry old man sitting on a throne, who judged our every thought and deed and wrote it down in a big book. That book would be used to prosecute our every failing, and we'd be eternally punished for our very existence on this planet. The alternative was to endlessly repent for our sins and to accept Jesus as our Lord and Savior. But given the pastor's fiery assurances of eternal damnation, even that didn't seem good enough.

It was fear-based religion, rooted in sick, distorted, pathological projections of patriarchal domination, guilt, and punishment.

As a youth, I read the high ideas espoused by Yeshua (Jesus) in the canonical gospels—"judge not that you be not judged," "as you forgive so shall you be forgiven," "do unto others as you would have them do unto you," "love your neighbor as yourself," and so on, but that's not what I experienced in daily life.

Coming of age in the turbulent years of the 1960's and 1970's, those high ideas didn't seem to get much "real world" application. I struggled to understand what was wrong with people, and really, what the whole thing (i.e., life) was all about. I began to focus on making sense of my own explorations and experiences instead of what my culture told me to believe, and I began to come to my own conclusions.

Seeing the immense disparity in what people experienced in life, it was obvious that relatively few would achieve the wealth, fame, or "beauty" that were then the contemporary measures of success, I reasoned that whatever life is about, it must apply to everyone. I deduced that the common denominator throughout the human experience *is the experience itself.* That conclusion alone helped relieve some of the judgmentalism of my early religious indoctrination.

Even though we seemed to view ourselves as the epitome of human achievement, the war, tensions, and strife of the day completely belied that notion. For that reason, I came to the conclusion that humanity was still in a relatively low state of evolutionary development. Yes, we could put one of our kind on the moon, but back on earth we were still bombing our own planet. What "intelligent" species would do that? Indeed, what intelligent species would bomb *any* planet?

The missing piece in those early conclusions was something that wasn't missing at all. I was looking for intellectual solutions to provide answers that could only be resolved by *heart.* Focused on *understanding,* I missed my own *beingness*—that individuated Awareness that we bury under layer upon layer of names, labels, and values as part of the human experience.

I understand now that is all "part of the ride" of being a human. That conundrum between *what we are* and *what we experience* appears to be the catalyst that drives the evolution of the collective consciousness.

"The Gospel of One: The Metaphysics of Revolution" is therefore a record of my journey from those early high ideas of Yeshua to the broader expansion of the collective consciousness, and hopefully some valid strategies for how we might better facilitate that evolution.

For those who disagree with my conclusions, I encourage your consideration of a motto frequently heard in twelve step support groups: "Take what you like and leave the rest."

As you love one another, so do you love Me.
As you love the earth, the moon, and the sun in the sky, so
do you love Me.
As you love all that is manifest creation, so do you love Me.

Introduction

This book is organized into four sections:

The Verses - Inspired words received during a time in which meditation was a major focus of my day.

Ten Essays - Ten essays that expound on the meaning of the Verses, and their metaphysical ramifications in relationship to the evolution/revolution/expansion of Consciousness currently occurring on the planet.

Living The Gospel of One - A thirty-day plan to study and practice The Gospel of One.

Addendums - Additional practices, scriptural references cited in the text (as indicated by brackets), a short glossary, and questions for the author.

With One Thought
Creation Sang.

The Verses

I am the voice that calls My Name.

The Verses

The verses are grouped as they appear in the text and are numbered solely for reference purposes. There is no hierarchy of revelation.

1. *In the beginning, I wondered,*
2. *What would it be like to be Many?*
3. *With One Thought*
4. *Creation Sang.*
5. *What we have here then*
6. *Is Me, experiencing SELF*
7. *As the One that is Many*
8. *And the Many that are One.*

9. *Descend now to the world of flesh*
10. *And for a time become Man*
11. *As error may lead to truth*
12. *And truth may lead to error*
13. *Discern that which has value*
14. *From that which has not.*

15. *I am the Voice that calls My Name.*

16. *We are the One that has chosen to experience Many.*
17. *We are the Many that are One.*
18. *We are Infinite, Immortal, and Indivisible Wholeness.*

19. *I am Source, the Absolute, the IS, the I AM that creates everything.*
20. *There is no thing apart from Me, and no thing that is not Me.*

21. *I, composed of nothing*
22. *Shape the stars*
23. *Beneath my feet.*

24. *I am the Source that is Many, the Many that are One.*

25. *I am One, the I AM,*
26. *Self-Creation and Source of Infinite Being.*
27. *Everywhere I look*
28. *I see me.*
29. *With every breath*
30. *I am this.*
31. *With whom shall I be angry?*
32. *Whom shall I attack?*

33. With whom shall I seek vengeance?
34. I am You, My Beloved.
35. There is no 'other'.

36. In the beginning, there was God.
37. God is Love.
38. Nothing has changed.

39. When I was young
40. I slew my brothers
41. And ravished my sisters.
42. I tore at the earth with fury
43. And cursed all that was before me.
44. Dead to Spirit, Blind to Life
45. Naught I saw but the torment
46. Of my own reflection.

47. We are the Answer
48. To the Promise
49. Of all we came to Be.

50. The universe knows what it is doing
51. The Godself is not amiss.
52. We are the Light
53. That creates the heavens
54. The love that guides the stars.

55. *From Wholeness I Am.*

56. *As you love one another, so do you love Me.*

57. *As you love the earth, the moon, and the sun in the sky, so do you love Me.*

58. *As you love all that is manifest creation, so do you love Me.*

59. *Comes a great calamity,*

60. *A necessary passage for the evolution of consciousness.*

61. *All look to the skies and ask,*

62. *"What have we wrought?"*

63. *From the Ashes, the Arising, the New Genesis of Man.*

64. *"These are the wages of our self-indulgence and fear,"*

65. *Cry the Sons of Man.*

66. *"Never again. Never again shall we fall."*

67. *All hearts rise to the new paradigm*

68. *Old Earth shall be no more.*

69. *Amid despair, find Purpose.*

70. *Amid chaos, find Clarity.*

71. *Amid fear, find Resolve.*

72. *Amid calamity, find Community.*

73. *I am Adam*

74. *I am Eve*

75. *The Gospel of One*

76. *The New Genesis of Man*

77. *I am the Source that is Many*

78. *The Many that are One.*

79. *Free of illusion*

80. *I Am All.*

81. *I am the storm, the wind, the rain*

82. *Fear nothing; embrace everything*

83. *This is Creation.*

84. *This is Life.*

85. *Where One Heart is true*

86. *Others may follow.*

87. *Now is the time to redeem all that has become before.*

88. *Forgive Everything*

89. *Love All*

90. *Trust Creation.*

With every breath
I am this.

Ten Essays

Discern that which has value
From that which has not.

1. In the Beginning

1. In the beginning, I wondered,

2. What would it be like to be Many?

3. With One Thought

4. Creation Sang.

5. What we have here then

6. Is Me, experiencing SELF

7. As the One that is Many

8. And the Many that are One.

The universe wants to tell a story. That story is the evolution of consciousness, in all its glory and madness. Earth is an adventure created to experience separation, to learn, and to participate in the evolution of consciousness at this level of existence.

As individualized experiences of the One Awareness, we incarnated into these specific bodies, to be born into our families of origin, to grow up in our towns and neighborhoods, and to participate in all of the mistakes, injustices, and tragedies that life brings our way.

The immortal Awareness embraces the manifest drama in all its goodness, badness, rightness, wrongness, triumph, and failure. The progression of consciousness is tracked not in a straight line, but by innumerable stumbling "missteps." Such seeming deviations are not errors, but necessary evolutions along the experiential path of creation.

All is well. We come here not only to ascend, but also to descend, not only to climb, but also to fall, not only to live, but also to die. We come to the Earth to experience the whole meal, not just the dessert.

We evolve in response to the demands of our life experience. In the absence of those demands, we adapt to a lower state of existence. Restrict the movement of a limb, and it atrophies. Sit on the couch in front of the television all day, and our stupor becomes stupid. If the body thinks it is no longer needed, then it declines, and so it is with hearts and minds.

Without suffering, there is no will to change. Without the irritation of the sand, the mollusk does not produce the beauty of the pearl. Challenges to our survival or well-being force us to respond, to evolve beyond the current situation. When the "comfort zone" of things as they are becomes too uncomfortable, we are forced to get off the couch, to ask new questions, to find new ways of thinking, to seek different answers, and to connect with resources that wouldn't have been accessed any other way.

We are not slaves to our circumstances, but active participants in the evolution of our species and life on Earth.

9. Descend now to the world of flesh
10. And for a time become Man
11. As error may lead to truth
12. And truth may lead to error
13. Discern that which has value
14. From that which has not.

Practice: *"Everything plays a part in the Evolution of Consciousness."*

Why are we here? Youth fades. Beauty is subjective. Fame is fleeting. Wealth corrupts. Power corrodes. Success is temporary. By what measure then, shall we determine our purpose?

Surely, if there is a reason for our presence in this world then it must be applicable to everyone. And so it is.

As the One who has chosen to experience the Many, the most fundamental purpose of our existence on this planet is simply to experience life as human beings. In that mission— no matter what happens—we can never fail. The same may be said for all the creatures with whom we share this planet—a bird is the One that is Many experiencing life as a bird, a cat is the One that is Many experiencing life as a cat, and so on.

But human beings are here to do more than experience life. The struggles and efforts of our human existence are a catalyst by which the universe evolves consciousness. Sometimes that "evolution" may seem like the folly of fools. Sometimes it may appear as unfortunate outcomes, showing us what we need to do better.

Like a fish in the ocean that can only discern its immediate environment, our everyday perception is limited to only a fragment of the larger processes that guide our existence. Whether seen or unseen, everything that happens writes a line, a paragraph, or a page in the story of the greater Evolution.

As we encounter the people and situations that manifest in our experiences throughout the day, make a conscious effort to remember that no matter the circumstances, *"Everything plays a part in the Evolution of Consciousness."*

2. From Wholeness

15. I am the Voice that calls My Name.

It is said, "There are many paths up the mountain."

There is no such mountain.

It is said, "All paths lead to the same place."

All paths lead to Here and Now.

Heaven is not an address. Bliss is not a thought. Awakening is not a scripture. The only thing between heaven/bliss/awakening and ourselves is everything we believe—all the mental constructions, models, and ultimate fictions of what we believe to be true.

The pursuit of "Enlightenment" can become a false paradigm; a misleading pseudo-task that challenges us to be something other than what we are. The problem—if there were one—is that we already believe that we are something we are not. We imagine that we are individual beings co-existing with other individual beings in a world constructed of more-or-less independent parts that somehow work together.

The paradox of our situation is that we are already that which we seek. How can One acquire that which One already Is?

16. We are the One that has chosen to experience Many.

17. We are the Many that are One.

18. We are Infinite, Immortal, and Indivisible Wholeness.

We are not separate from creation; we are creation. We are as much a part of this universe as the earth beneath our feet or the gravitational tides that shape the stars. This is our home. This is our playground. This is the body of God made manifest throughout all creation.

The issue, should we choose to pursue it, is to wake up from the dream that we are separate from everything else.

Practice: *Experience the Peace of God that defies Understanding*

All the madness in the world is in our heads—in our imaginations and beliefs, whereas the physical world in which we live is in a state of unending, unified perfection as determined by the laws of physics. The physical reality is that All is Well. Everything happens exactly as it is supposed to happen according to the natural laws of the universe, regardless of whether we agree with the results.

"What is" is infinitely greater than anything we can think about it, but no further away than the beating of our own hearts. *To find God, stop looking. Stop looking, and start Being.* The more we release the illusions and false attachments in our minds, the more we experience that "the Kingdom of God is within you." [1]

Meditation is the art of waking up from the world of our imaginations and beliefs. There are many ways to meditate. We may simply follow our breath as we focus on our inhalations and exhalations. We may chant; recite prayers or mantras; practice specific breathing rhythms; use prayer beads; listen to binaural beats or guided visualizations; utilize virtual reality programs, do walking meditations or other "mindfulness" practices.

The key to learning meditation is to 1) keep it simple and 2) begin. Find a method that works and allow the technique to evolve as the practice deepens. To establish a practice, a few minutes a day on a consistent basis will prove more resourceful than the occasional attempt. Five minutes is sufficient to begin. The goal is for meditation to become a habit, not an endurance contest. Meditation times will naturally lengthen as the practice deepens.

A Simple Meditation:

As with anything new, this may feel awkward at first but becomes easier with practice.

NOTE: This method uses nasal breathing for both inhalations and exhalations. Other methods emphasize breathing in through the nose and out through the mouth. Do whichever works best for you.

Start your timer if you are using one.

Sit upright in a chair with your feet on the floor, or in any position that supports good posture.

To begin, sit relaxed. Place one open palm high across your upper chest (just below the suprasternal notch between the shoulder blades), and inhale deeply through your nose. Feel the expansion of your chest and your lower belly as you inhale. Hold the breath for a few seconds and then exhale slowly and fully through the nose, allowing your shoulders to sink into a more relaxed pose. Repeat for a total of three inhalations and exhalations.

Now sit erect with good posture. Lower your chin a bit so that the neck muscles relax. Place your hands in your lap, the back of one hand resting in the palm of the other, or alternatively rest the hands on the thighs, palms up for receptivity, or palms down for grounding.

Close your eyes.

Breathe in and out through your nose, with the mouth lightly closed (the jaws should be relaxed, not clenched). NOTE: There are several advantages to nasal breathing, among which is an increase in the production of nitric oxide, which dilates blood vessels and thereby lowers blood pressure and increases oxygenation.

Sit quietly. With relaxed focus, follow the rhythm of your breath. Focus on the in-and-out flow of air through your nostrils, or the slight rise and fall of your chest, or the gentle expansion and relaxation of your lower belly. The point is to focus on the present moment, whatever it may be. This is about flow, not force.

Without strain, slow your breathing so that the time between respirations is gradually extended.

Thoughts will come. Do not judge or criticize yourself. The mind generates thoughts simply because that is what it does. As soon as you become aware that you are thinking, simply return focus to your breath. This cycle may repeat dozens or even hundreds of times depending on the length of the meditation. Any awareness of the resumption of thoughts is an indication of progress, not failure.

As thoughts arise, it may be helpful to once again place an open palm high across your upper chest, breathing slowly and deeply several times. Feel the air as it expands your thoracic cavity from the lungs all the way down to the lower abdomen. Exhale slowly and fully. Maintain the posture and repeat as long as needed to help calm the mind.

If especially discordant thoughts intrude, open your eyes and look straight ahead. While keeping your head stationary and your eyes on the same horizontal plane, move your eyes back-and-forth from extreme left to extreme right, without strain. Resume meditation as the thoughts recede.

With practice, the interval between thoughts will lengthen. These seemingly empty spaces or gaps become experiences of profound peace.

When the timer sounds, turn it off. Rest quietly for a short while, or return to meditation if you wish.

If you feel at all "spacey" or ungrounded when you rise, walk around and lightly stomp your feet a few times.

Meditation allows us to experience a state of consciousness where truly, "All is well." The more we meditate, the more we find peace, and the less anything else disturbs us. We may discover that "heaven" is not so much a place we may go when we die, but a state of being that is right here, right now, and a place we never left. This is the meaning of, "...unless a man be born again [born into a new awareness], he cannot see the Kingdom of God." [2] This is the pearl of such exquisite quality that the gem dealer sold everything he had to obtain it. [3]

Any spiritual practice that does not include some form of meditation is a mere shadow of what it could be.

Just for today, *"Experience the peace of God that defies understanding."* [4]

3. Source

19. I am Source, the Absolute, the IS, the I AM that creates
everything.
20. There is no thing apart from Me, and no thing that is
not Me.

There are absolute truths, and there are relative truths. An absolute truth is I AM. Relative truths are at least as numerous as sentient beings in the universe. Indeed, the universe is God experiencing Self as Many—every plant, animal, person, particle, and conscious entity. This is the *Godself*.

Everyone and everything emanate from—and always remain within—Source. Source might also be called God, Allah, Shiva, Brahman, The Is, The Absolute, All That Is, the I AM, The One that is Many, the One Awareness, or any other label that describes the absolute reality from which everything proceeds.

21. I, composed of nothing
22. Shape the stars
23. Beneath my feet.

Source is both everything and "nothing" (i.e., not a separate thing), because in absolute terms there is no-thing else. For that reason, it is said, "From nothingness [no-thing-ness] comes everything."

24. I am the Source that is Many, the Many that are One.

Separation is a perception created by Mind. Separation allows our individualized awareness within *Godself* to savor the play of yin/yang dualities of consciousness: good/bad, black/white, right/wrong, them/us, and so on. Neither distinction exists without the other. There is no "up" without "down."

The egoic-mind runs like an automated software program that continually seeks contrasts and relationships. What is different? What is useful? How is it related to anything else? Essentially, "How may the current set of sensory data be interpreted to enhance survival?"

If the information appears to be routine—that is, has no new or significant impact to survival—the mind drifts elsewhere. This is how we arrive at our destination with no recollection of the commute. We tune out the route because we've seen it hundreds of times before; but introduce something new—a loud noise, sudden movement, or an attractive stranger—and we quickly focus on the moment and assess the new stimulus.

We construct internal models of the world based on our perceptions. Those models are necessarily limited by the relative bandwidth of our senses, our instrumentation, and our thought processes.

We collect understandings along the way and use these to inform the possibilities and limits of our lives. Indeed, without intervention, the interpretations and decisions we acquire at a very young age may play out repetitiously for an entire lifetime.

Separation creates the illusion that we are apart from one another, apart from the world we inhabit, and apart from Source. A wave crests on the ocean and we interpret it as a singular event. Yet, in a moment, it is re-absorbed into the whole and is seemingly gone. Shall we then mourn its loss, celebrate its remembrance, or desire another that is even more spectacular?

Snared in duality, our emotions swell and fall with our judgments and expectations, yet all waves are essentially the same: water, wind, and tide create energy in motion. Focused on what was, we miss what is. Distracted by the narrow spectrum of our thoughts and desires, we miss the opportunity to appreciate the now.

In the absence of awareness of other modes of consciousness, we come to falsely identify ourselves with ego-mind. In separation, each person becomes the center of a self-important universe around which all-else orbits. Problems are externalized, as are solutions. The challenges we experience and the answers we seek, it seems, are forever located without, never within.

Yet, within Source there is no-thing seemingly outside of us that is not also us. The resolution we seek is not an external object or experience, but participation in the evolution of our own consciousness. There is no-thing apart from God, and that includes each of us. This is the meaning of, "I and my Father are One." [5]

Practice: *"No one is better than anyone else. No one is less."*

We are that which created us. Every aspect of creation manifests within the context of template and role, but all emanate from Source. We are individualized explorations of the same field of consciousness. We are all the same soup. There are none less than us, and none greater.

The people we despise are no lesser acts of God than those whom we adore. From the most miserable among us to the most exalted, *Godself* plays many roles, but is none of them and all of them.

All hierarchies are contrived. One particle of matter is no better than any other part. Rank and status are the stuff of pretense and perception.

No one is better than anyone else. No one is worse. No one is more important. No one is less. In the sight of God, the person who mops the floor is as beloved as the person who sits behind the executive's desk, a leader is no greater than a citizen, and the student is no less than the master.

Our differences are objects of perception, not Love. God's Love is unconditional; therefore it is equal to all.

Just for today, as we go about our daily business, notice personalities that we might ordinarily judge as greater or less than ourselves. These might be authority figures at our place of work or school, homeless or disadvantaged people we encounter on the street, politicians, "sports heroes," or celebrities we see in the media. In each case, be mindful that, *"No one is better than anyone else; no one is less."*

4. My Beloved

25. I am One, the I AM,

26. Self-Creation and Source of Infinite Being.

27. Everywhere I look

28. I see me.

29. With every breath

30. I am this.

31. With whom shall I be angry?

32. Whom shall I attack?

33. With whom shall I seek vengeance?

34. I am You, My Beloved.

35. There is no 'other'.

Source is unfiltered Bliss, which might also be described as Love. Love without condition, without judgment, and without condemnation.

We could also say:

36. In the beginning, there was God.

37. God is Love.

38. Nothing has changed.

God is not angry, not jealous, and not vengeful. God is All There Is, therefore with whom could She be angry, but Self?

As children, we might form an image of God as an angry old man on a throne, a sort of omnipresent Santa Claus that records "who's naughty and nice," and dispenses rewards or punishments according to our behavior. This is God as all-powerful, knows-it-all, angry father. This is God as cosmic boogey-man, waiting to strike us down.

These are obsolete projections of patriarchal domination, guilt, and punishment. All are rooted in the same basic misunderstandings that:

1) God is somewhere else,

2) Man is separate from God,

3) Man is separate from nature, and

4) Individuals are separate from mankind as a whole.

These erroneous beliefs are created by the mind's ability to discern hierarchies and divisions where none truly exist. God is not somewhere else, but within the heart of our own Awareness, no further away than the disappearance of our own illusions. No living thing is independent of the larger universe that nurtures its existence. No suffering is beyond the reach of our own empathy and compassion.

We are all the same soup.

The only separation between Man and God or anything else is the mind's ability to create contrasts. In terms of our physical survival, this is an essential ability that helps identify what is safe and what is not safe. In a manner of speaking, it is a database of information that allows us to react without additional exploration or thought. We see a peach and somewhere in the database it says, "That may be good to eat." We see a scorpion and reflexively move away because "it stings." We don't have to taste the peach or touch the scorpion to know how these objects of perception may benefit or harm our well-being.

Our perceptions are subject to bias, incomplete information, misinterpretation, and unconscious revision. In the early days of computer programming, it was said, "Garbage in, garbage out." This means that erroneous data fed into a program creates erroneous results. And so it is with our belief systems.

The so-called "Fall of Man" is simply a judgment applied to the illusion of separation within the survival mechanisms of our own mind. The "original sin" was not eating from the tree of knowledge, but the perception of contrasts within awareness. The "shame" of our "nakedness" in the Garden of Eden is a projection of guilt created within our own consciousness. It has no external source.

"The Fall of Man" never happened.

There is no "original sin."

Shame and guilt are inventions of the human experience.

Within *Godself*—within God experiencing Self—there is no difference between what is seemingly outside of us and what is seemingly inside of us. It is all the same thing—Us. It cannot be otherwise. There is no-thing else.

Everywhere we look, *"I see me."* Every expression of beauty or seeming horror, *"I am this."* Everyone we adore, everyone we seemingly despise, *"I am You, My Beloved."*

The frequency of God is Love, Now, Forever, and Always.

God does not judge us. *We judge ourselves,* and we act out that judgment across time.

What goes into collective consciousness must play out through collective consciousness. Every wrong, every injury, every infliction of harm and villainy is to ourselves. There is no one else. Guilt demands condemnation. Condemnation calls for punishment. Punishment inspires resentment. Resentment leads to retaliation. Retaliation inspires more condemnation, and on it goes. This is the meaning of, "Judge not that you be not judged; for as you judge, so shall you be judged." [6]

Practice: *"I do not need to judge this."*

Whatever our seeming differences, we are more alike than dissimilar. We all share the same needs, wants, and fears. We all have the same basic requirements for physical survival (air, water, food, shelter, sleep, community). We all crave sustenance at multiple levels of our being. We want to belong, to be valued, to be recognized, to be respected, to be part of something bigger than ourselves. We all fear loss, abandonment, powerlessness, and death.

From the aspect of *Godself,* other beings are simply different expressions of the One that has chosen to experience

Many. The persons or groups we despise are ultimately as much a part of the human experiment as everyone else. Minimally, even the worst behavior may reveal what we need to change within our families, societies, ideologies, or the workings of our own mind. Even as we must sometimes protect ourselves from the harmful conduct of others, we might also be grateful it is they, and not us, that are acting out such discordant roles within consciousness.

Projections of criticism, blame, and guilt are a form of personal and collective self-harm. When we are angry, disapprove of another, or hate, who feels those emotions more intimately than anyone else? We do. Whose blood pressure goes up? The objects of our derision may or may not be consciously aware of our disdain, but the physiological and psychological effects are intimately experienced within our own being.

Just for today, practice non-judgment. For our own health and peace of mind, release the need to project labels and values onto persons or events. If there is a safety or health concern, correct it without the need to project blame and guilt. If there is a problem, fix it without the need to vilify the circumstances. Set the drama aside, allow the situation to be what it is, and do what needs to be done.

Remember, our judgments resolve nothing, but only create further disturbances within consciousness.

Just for today, as we become aware of our projections of disapproval onto personalities, situations, and events, practice the idea, *"I do not need to judge this."*

5. To Change the World

39. When I was young

40. I slew my brothers

41. And ravished my sisters.

42. I tore at the earth with fury

43. And cursed all that was before me.

44. Dead to Spirit, Blind to Life

45. Naught I saw but the torment

46. Of my own reflection.

All aggression is based on an illusion, an egoic projection that there is another to blame, conquer, or attack. The basis of aggression is the fear of loss—some perceived compromise to survival, identity, power, or control. The ego projects guilt and attack on whomever or whatever it chooses to blame for how itself has chosen to feel or think. The object of those perceptions feels threatened and pushes back. The cycle of fear, attack, and retribution continues until tension is released and some semblance of balance is restored. That, or the parties withdraw into states of charged toxicity with further disturbances to individual and group consciousness.

The underlying basis of the overwhelming majority of what is perceived to be "wrong with the world" is only a thought—mere nonsense that the ego has made up. You did that to me, therefore I must do this to you. For some to have more, others must have less. If only I had what I want, I would be safe; I would be happy; I would be fulfilled. My need justifies your suffering. Those who do not believe as we do must be feared; must be devalued; must be defeated; must be eliminated. Our way is the right way; your way is an aberration. "God" loves us more; "God" loves you less.

What is "wrong" with the world? It is simply the cause-and-effect of our thoughts, acts, and intentions; in other words, karma.

We think of "karma" as a system of individual rewards and punishments based on moral principles, but this is a limited, egocentric understanding. Karma is impersonal. It does not judge right or wrong; it is simply a feedback mechanism that delivers results.

We might interpret karma to mean that if we squash a gnat with our finger that at some future time we will reborn as a gnat to be crushed, or suffer some equivalent punishment, but this is an immature understanding. From the perspective of the One experiencing the Many, we are already the gnat. Effectively, in squashing the gnat we killed an expression of the same Being that is Us.

At its most elemental, karma is the expression of the desire of the One to experience the Many. This desire creates the universe. It is the answer to the question, "If I do this, what happens?" As such, everyone and everything is a manifestation of the simultaneous flow of cause-and-effect within the experiences of *Godself*.

Essentially, karma is a living, dynamic composition that plays out across time and circumstance. It is an individual matter only within the context of the overall collective expression. Whether I walk down the street with a gruff attitude or a courteous smile, it affects not only myself but also everyone I encounter. It is not so much, "As you sow, so shall *you* reap," but, "As *we* sow, so shall *we* reap." [7]

Within the collective experience of One—and that is all there is—karmic "justice" begins immediately. There is no delay between cause-and-effect. Whether I strike my brother with a fist or explode a bomb over his village, "I" as *Godself* immediately suffer the consequences of those actions, with repercussions that may reverberate across generations.

The injuries and devastation may seemingly play out through someone else's experience, but within *Godself*, there is no one else. As physical beings, we could not survive if our nervous systems were wired together with those of the animals we have relied upon for sustenance. Even so, if our hearts are open, the suffering of no being is beyond the reach of our empathy and compassion, and the impact of our deeds no further than our own conscience.

Practice: *"Kindness."*

Karma may be thought of as a neutral feedback loop within the evolution of consciousness. It simply produces some version of what we put into it. The obvious lesson is that what we do as individuals affects who we are and the results we obtain as a group. Conversely, what groups do affects who we are and the results we obtain as individuals. As both individuals and as a collective, we create the environment in which everyone lives. This is the meaning of, "Do unto others as you would have them do unto you." As we do unto others, *we are doing unto ourselves.* [8]

In terms of physics, all behavior is neutral. That is, the physical laws of the universe do not keep track of "who is naughty and nice," but simply define how the universe works.

However, in terms of our experience, not all behavior is skillful, or resourceful. The question then becomes, "How may we obtain more skillful (more resourceful) results?"

The fact is we could change the world for the better in a single day. What if, one morning, all around the world, people woke up and simply decided to do the right thing? Certainly, there might be multiple and even conflicting opinions of what the "right thing" is, but surely everyone could agree to simply do no harm. In itself, that would dramatically change the world for the better—in just twenty-four hours!

Doing the right thing is not complicated; it is heart-based. In practice, it is love, compassion, non-judgment, forgiveness, non-violence, tolerance, community, ecology, patience, courtesy, respect, and cooperation. This is the essence of, "Love your neighbor as yourself." [9]

In a single word, the "right thing" is simply kindness.

Kindness is the natural expression of the divine Being we truly are, rather than the egotistical monstrosities that we sometimes allow ourselves to become.

To change the world for the better, practice kindness. Be courteous. Respect others. Respect the planet. Release the need to judge, to condemn, or to vilify. Right now, just for today, *practice kindness in whatever form or opportunities present themselves to you.*

6. Clearing Karma

47. We are the Answer
48. To the Promise
49. Of all we came to Be

We come to the Earth not as a blank slate, but as an individuated Awareness with an agenda for its own role in the evolution of consciousness. That Awareness seeks balance for its experience in previous incarnations including the resolution of problematic themes that have carried forth across the ages.

As intuitive, interconnected beings, we then take on additional thought forms—beliefs and karmic patterns—that often do not belong to us. For example, we may have grown up in an environment where a parent struggled with his or her own karmic baggage, and through the process of imitation ("monkey see, monkey do") re-created that pattern within ourselves.

Multiply this interaction across large groups of people, among nations, and across the illusion of time, and we see how karma—the neutral play of cause and effect—manifests through the collective consciousness.

The sum total of all experiences are contained within the consciousness of *Godself*. As the Many, we are everyone who is alive, has lived, or shall ever be, and all the experiences of those manifestations. We are good; we are bad; we are right; we are wrong; and we are all possible permutations of those qualities. We are the most admirable heroes, and the most despicable villains. We are the people we fear, the people we hate, and the people we harm.

Every insane, heinous act that anyone has ever committed occurred within the collective awareness of *Godself*.

Why do people do bad things? The simplest answer is, because they can. In criminological terms, it is a function of means, motive, and opportunity. We could also say that the perpetrators have no emotional, ethical, moral, or physical barriers against engaging in such behavior.

Bad behavior is also an indication of the Awareness level of the individual or group. In low awareness states of egoic identity, we have little appreciation for how our activities affect anyone or anything that we ourselves do not care about. We stumble around in our illusions, indifferent to the consequences of our behavior until some manifestation of pain and suffering demands our attention.

In low awareness states we don't know who we are. We think we are the construction of beliefs and memories within the egoic mind. We imagine that we are separate from the whole, and therefore our actions have little consequence outside of what we see as our narrow range of concern. We literally do not understand what we are doing. This is the basis of the expression, "Forgive them, Father, for they know not what they do." [10]

Our life experiences also twist us in unpredictable ways. Some become saints, some become psychopaths. We hold anger, frustration, and resentments we may not know how to resolve. We operate in states of "diminished capacity" because we are distracted, we are exhausted, or haven't had the experiences that would allow us to make better choices. The point is, whether consciously or unconsciously, we are not always at our best, nor are the people or beings we encounter.

Taking all of the elements that allow bad behavior as a whole, we could say that bad behavior is a pattern of information. If we take away any of those elements, we have the possibility to change the overall pattern.

If we want "better people" in the world we have to create the conditions for better people to occur. Imagine what a different world we might have if our children were taught empathy, respect for life, and mutually beneficial cooperation as much as any of the other subjects in their schooling. Imagine a world inspired by the Spirit of "We" not "me."

What shall we do with ourselves? How do we escape from the cycle of anger, attack, and retribution? How do we transcend the play of karma? In any given situation, what can we do to help create the best possible outcome?

When bad behavior occurs, we might consider a three-tiered response:

1. Stop the damage. When something bad happens, we have a natural tendency to focus on who or what to blame, but legal or liability issues can be determined at another time. In situations where health or safety are at risk, our focus should be on preventing further damage and assisting the injured. Health and safety first, finger-pointing later.

In cases of extreme violence, stopping the damage may mean isolating or neutralizing the causative factor. Every living creature is entitled to act in the interests of its own self-preservation, and in the absence of other options, there is no "sin" in legitimate self-defense. The most loving thing we can do for everyone involved is to stop perpetrators from doing more harm.

2. Dissipate the Energy. Bad behavior offends our sense of fair play. We want justice. We want retribution. We want revenge. The conundrum is this: If someone is pouring poison into the well, pouring more poison into the well is not going to help the village, and so it is with the collective consciousness. In other words, we must resist the temptation to respond to bad behavior with more bad behavior, especially if the response is disproportionate to the original stimulus.

Dissipating the energy may mean being "the only adult in the room," working to calm the discordant energy, remaining silent as others shout, choosing the least injurious response, or simply walking away.

3. Transform the Outcome. To transform the outcome of a situation we can: Heal the injured, restore well-being to the traumatized, rebuild infrastructure, honor the sacrifice of the lost, and implement whatever life-affirming lessons may be gleaned from the events. We can help clear discordant energy from the collective consciousness by forgiving all of the personalities involved. This does not mean allowing the harmful activities of others to continue or allowing them to escape appropriate repercussions. It means not magnifying the discordant energy further within consciousness.

Practice: *Forgiveness*

The universe is NOT a grand morality play of "good" versus "evil." It is a self-evolving exploration of consequences. It is the answer to the question, "If I do this, what happens?"

We have come to the Earth not to escape karma for the purpose of our singular advancement, but to transform consciousness through the evolution of our mutual being. As we go about our lives today and challenging situations arise, we can make conscious choices about how we respond.

In any situation, we have the choice not to react in a destructive way. As we release our negative reactions, we render obsolete the disruptive pattern of karma that would otherwise have occurred. We can refuse to blame others for our thoughts and feelings. We can release the need for judgment, justification, fairness, and vengeance. We can drop our perception of personalities from an event and simply accept it as a pattern of discordant energy. We can forgive the other party, the situation, and ourselves. We can center ourselves in the now and remember to breathe (i.e., to simply be).

All "sins" will be forgiven by the people who perpetrated the offenses: Us.

Forgiveness is the art of clearing discordant energy from the collective consciousness. When we change our response, we change the people and world around us. Our conscious choice to act from a higher state of being breaks the chain of anger, attack, and retribution. This is the meaning of, "What you forgive on earth (individuated consciousness) will be forgiven in heaven (the collective consciousness of *Godself*)." [11]

Forgiveness allows us to release others to the consequences of their behavior without the need for further entanglement on our part. We don't have to carry that burden in our hearts or allow that "vibration" to grow within our consciousness.

Forgiveness frees our energy to rejoin the natural flow of events without the need to control the outcome. As we release the discordant energy patterns within ourselves, we also help release the associated karmic tension within *Godself*.

Often, it is difficult to catch ourselves before we react less resourcefully to an offending situation. A three-step process of forgiveness may help dispel the tension. Note: This procedure can be employed even though the situation has passed or the other parties are no longer present.

First, forgive the situation in exactly the terms with which you first responded. For example, if you responded by cursing the situation or 'other' personality with a derogatory name, forgive them in your own mind for "being" that image. This "validates" your emotional response without suppressing it. Effectively, it takes the first bit of emotional charge away from the situation.

For example, "I forgive this situation for being awful," or "I forgive [that person] for being awful."

Secondly, forgive yourself for labeling the situation or person in that manner:

"I forgive myself for labeling this situation awful," or "I forgive myself for labeling [that person] awful."

Lastly, forgive yourself for your lack of patience with the situation or person:

"I forgive myself for my lack of patience with this situation," or "I forgive myself for my lack of patience with that person."

Effectively, we are forgiving ourselves twice and the situation or the other party once. Why are we forgiving ourselves twice and the other party only once? The other party may not be aware that their behavior was offensive, or they may simply not care. Consequently, it is ourselves that may most acutely feel the consequences of the offense.

The point of the process is to dispel the discord within ourselves. We don't need to store it in our minds, as physical tension in our bodies, or as karmic tension in the collective consciousness.

Just for today, forgive the unpleasant situations or personalities you encounter, and forgive your response to those events.

Life does not travel in straight lines. We think it is supposed to go this way or that way, but the truth is that it goes all over the place, and we never know what is going to happen or where we may end up. Indeed, we may be the person who creates an unpleasant situation in someone else's experience!

Life is messy. Forgiveness helps clean up the mess, whether it belongs to ourselves or to the collective consciousness of humanity. *Just for today, practice forgiveness.*

7. As You Love One Another

50. The universe knows what it is doing

51. The Godself is not amiss.

52. We are the Light

53. That creates the heavens

54. The love that guides the stars.

Separation is a story we tell ourselves to facilitate the experience of the Many among the One. This is a function that the body and the ego do very well. As biological organisms our primary imperatives are to survive and to reproduce. We will tolerate almost any conditions in order to survive, and we will attempt to reproduce in defiance of all moral and social conventions. Meanwhile, the ego says, "I need to feel that I belong, that I am valued, and that my existence makes a difference in this world."

If these cravings for sustenance are not satisfied—to survive, to belong, to procreate, to be important to someone or something—we attempt to fill them some other way, become *dis-eased*, or shut ourselves down to numb the pain of our existence.

Who we think we are is an assemblage of perceptions, understandings, and memories accumulated over time.

Essentially, it is a pattern of belief. Likewise, so are our views of the world and other beings. These beliefs are a form of mental shorthand intended to simplify our survival, but are never the things themselves. Instead, they become a filter through which we experience our lives.

We see a tree outside our window and unless there is something unusual or striking in its appearance, scarcely "see" it at all because we already know what "tree" looks like. Our internal database recognizes the pattern and gives it no further attention.

Arguably, we hardly experience the objects of our perception. What we experience are the models of those objects that we have accumulated in our heads. Those models include labels and values—good, bad, tall, short, fat, skinny, ugly, pretty, and so on—that significantly color our perceptions.

We largely live in a dream state of our own creation. Captured by our desires, ensnared by our attachments, we rise and fall with the pursuit of our expectations. Busy, busy, busy, forever busy, we rush to and fro with the urgency of our assignments. Oblivious to what may be right in front of our faces, we are hardly conscious but run on automatic pilot repeating the same patterns of thought and activities on a daily basis.

It is then little wonder that in terms of spiritual attainment, we think we need to be somewhere else, to do something else, to be someone else. We sense that we are not worthy and require the intervention of some external force to save us.

55. From Wholeness I Am.

56. As you love one another, so do you love Me.

57. As you love the earth, the moon, and the sun in the sky, so do you love Me.

58. As you love all that is manifest creation, so do you love Me.

Practice: *Love Everyone and Everything*

The fact is, we are addicted to the dream state. We are enslaved, at times, by the puffery of our self-importance. We become obsessed with the pursuit of our goals. We over-indulge ourselves through consumption and gratification. We glorify our heroes and vilify our enemies. We cling to our misery and run from our guilt. We rage against the world when it is not as we think it should be.

We are ensnared by the passions and travails of the human drama. This is not a mistake; it is our mission. The primary function of our existence is to experience the world as human beings. And yet, we sense that there is something more and that somehow we are "missing the mark" of our own being.

Seemingly caught somewhere between the holy and the profane, we ignore our divinity to experience our physicality and we suppress our corporeality to be more divine. How are we to find balance? What are we to do?

The solution is love; the gateway is compassion; the sacrament is gratitude. Finding our way is not about rules, it is about heart. It is not an intellectual understanding or a state of mind, but a state of being.

To experience Wholeness we must let go of division, including the divisiveness we feel within ourselves. It is only through our internal schisms that we project blame, conflict, guilt, and shame into the world.

To love one another we must fully love ourselves, love the earth, love all of the organisms and creatures that give life to this planet; love the sun, the moon, and the stars in the sky. To love everyone and everything is the true meaning of, "Love God with all your spirit, all your heart, and all your mind." [12]

Just for today, pause at random moments throughout the day to unconditionally express, "I love you," to at least five objects of your perception. These could be people, animals, plants, or inanimate objects in the environment.

It doesn't matter what the object is, because as the manifest body of the divine, the universe is God everywhere in all things at all times, and truly, *"Everywhere I look, I see Me."*

Our intention forms a loving connection to the objects of our perception. With continued practice, we come to love everyone and everything. Effectively, as incarnate beings we become Love.

Just for today, *practice Love.*

For additional ways to practice love, see "Practicing Love" in the Addendums.

8. Compassion

59. Comes a great calamity,

60. A necessary passage for the evolution of consciousness.

61. All look to the skies and ask,

62. "What have we wrought?"

63. From the Ashes, the Arising, the New Genesis of Man.

64. "These are the wages of our self-indulgence and fear,"

65. Cry the Sons of Man.

66. "Never again. Never again shall we fall."

67. All hearts rise to the new paradigm.

68. Old Earth shall be no more.

Cataclysmic events level the social playing field. When a storm reduces our town to rubble, the instincts of tribal and familial survival take precedence over the petty divisions of egoic consciousness. We don't care about the class, color, or bank balance of the hand that provides help when we lay buried under rubble. Nor do we care about the social standing of the person whom we help rescue. In such situations, we instinctively comfort one another to the best of our humanity.

Inevitable great calamities are coming. We take the Earth for granted. We respect nothing and consume everything. We poison the planet. We poison ourselves. We act with indifference toward our fellow beings. Everyone and everything become commodities to be used and discarded.

We may imagine that God will save us because we are the "good" people. Comforted by egoistic self-righteousness, those whom we think of as *less than us* will be "left behind" or condemned to an alternate dimension of endless torment. But what if "salvation" is not individual, but collective? What if "Earth school" is a lesson in *planetary responsibility*? What if the resolution of the turmoil within the collective consciousness is the catalyst by which the species evolves beyond the current discord?

Who will save us from the consequences of our behavior? Who will lead us away from the ashes of our self-destruction?

Consensual reality says that some must suffer so that others may prosper, that consumption, plunder, and waste are without limit; that those with whom we disagree are mortal enemies; that the beliefs we once held are what we should continue to believe, now and forever.

These are false, failed paradigms that cannot create a sustainable future. Nor can those of us in developed countries return to an idealized past that never existed for most human beings on this planet.

Doing different versions of the same things we have always done only perpetuates the same results. No matter what has happened in the past or how we have arrived at our present circumstance, our redemption is in the present moment and what we do now.

It is time to write a new script.

"One generation abandons the enterprises of another like stranded vessels," wrote American transcendentalist Henry David Thoreau.

The politics of fear, hate, and division are obsolete. We do not need to overthrow governments, assassinate officials, burn buildings, or tear down institutions or groups. We do not need a riot in the streets; we need a riot in our hearts. We are the revolution we seek—a revolution within consciousness.

That revolution is as simple, and as complex, as this:

1) Let go of the past.

It is time to abandon the "stranded vessels" of fear, hate, anger, and greed.

It is time to transform the economies of consumption, plunder, and waste.

It is time to outgrow the "false idols" of self-importance and ego worship.

It is time to realize that there is only one boat and we are all in it.

This is the meaning of, "Let the dead bury the dead." Let the dead bury dead beliefs, dead ideas, dead personalities, and dead ways of doing things. [13]

2) Live in the now.

Meditation and other mindful practices allow us to clear our heads of the distractions created by mind. The more we experience the peace of our unfiltered awareness, the less we are subject to the egoistic delusions of our imagination.

3) Act from a higher state of being, with kindness, compassion, respect, and a broader sense of who we are and what we are doing here.

Practice: *Compassion*

Does an earthquake seek destruction? Does a hurricane intend harm? Is a tornado vengeful?

In simple terms, each of these events may be described as a release of energy to achieve a more balanced state, regardless of whether that is the redistribution of heat in the atmosphere or the release of tectonic energy beneath our feet. Natural disasters are not malevolent forces, but simply indifferent manifestations of how things work.

Each calamity, each upheaval, each re-balancing of tension—whether natural or man-made—offers us an opportunity, not only to do something different, but to do something better, to achieve a more beneficial utilization of our resources and to find more innovative solutions to our needs.

Recreating what we have done before can only produce similar results. Our power to obtain better results is in how we respond now.

Our present challenges are an immense opportunity to make our world a better place. There is nothing like a common threat to bring us together. There is nothing like direct suffering and pain to cut through the hubris and noise of our lives. There is nothing like a struggle for survival to focus on the things that really matter.

The problems and challenges we face are largely creations of our own design. We can find solutions to these problems, or ways to adapt, or workarounds to ameliorate their impact.

No one survives alone. There have always been challenges to our survival, and we have always overcome them. The challenges of our time are no different.

69. Amid despair, find Purpose.
70. Amid chaos, find Clarity.
71. Amid fear, find Resolve.
72. Amid calamity, find Community.

Eons ago, without fang or claw, that's how our ancestors survived the long night of the predator on the plains of Africa. We do not have any other choice than to solve the challenges to our survival, and to solve them together.

Life offers opportunities, but no guarantees. At some point in everyone's life, some great loss or devastating hardship will occur. We don't know what the gruff or angry people we encounter may have experienced. We don't know what heartache or tragedy those with a sour countenance may be suffering.

Just for today, *practice compassion*. Truly, "Do unto others as you would have them do unto you." Be courteous. Be kind. Be respectful. As opportunities to help present themselves, follow through. Like a pebble dropped into a pond, even small efforts may yield large results.

9. Adam and Eve

73. I am Adam

74. I am Eve

75. The Gospel of One

76. The New Genesis of Man

77. I am the Source that is Many

78. The Many that are One.

79. Free of illusion

80. I Am All.

In our mythologies and popular fictions, we imagine ourselves assailed by giant creatures of the earth, sea beasts, reptiles, apes, and so on. The exaggerated forms of these "monsters" are projections of our own primal fears of the things that lurk beneath the waves or in the darkness of night. As much as we may fear the colossal brutes of our imagination, the truth of the matter is that to all other life forms on earth *we are the monsters.*

We victimize our fellow creatures as though they were inanimate, unfeeling things, mere commodities to be used and discarded. We regard the earth as though it was nothing, a limitless dumping ground for exploitation and abuse. We poison, pollute, and attack our own planet with bombs. We poison, pollute, and attack ourselves.

Yet, we regard ourselves as the highest form of life on earth, the "pinnacle of God's creation," "made in God's own image," or perhaps more simply, "the top" of the food chain. [14]

We think that we are somehow above nature, but we are not. We are as enmeshed in our environment as any fish in a lake or stream. As physical beings we are not independent of our world, but fully dependent on it for our survival.

Perhaps a better measurement of evolutionary achievement is the ability of a species to live in harmony with its environment? From that perspective, we may find ourselves at the *bottom* of the evolutionary scale, not the top!

We could argue that the difference between ourselves and other animals is that we have a more highly evolved brain. Or we could argue that human beings have souls, whereas we want to believe that animals do not, but this is an egoic delusion.

We think we are better than everything else, but one particle of matter is no better than any other part. We are all the same soup. All creation is the expression of One Spirit: *"I am the Source that is Many, the Many that are One... Everywhere I look, I see me. With every breath, I am this."*

Within the consciousness of One Awareness, we are everyone alive, everyone who has ever lived, and everyone that shall ever be. Within the collective experience of duality, we are good, we are bad, we are right, and we are wrong. We are the most admirable heroes, and the most despicable villains. We are the people we love and the people we fear. We are both victim and perpetrator of our own crimes.

Consensual reality is an assemblage of information created by the egoic mind. The mind's ability to discern contrasts within the indivisible whole is a crucial survival skill, but is also the basis of the illusion of separation, the illusion that one part could be greater than any other part, and the illusion that the people we condemn or attack or exploit are not also Us. *We are the One that is Many and the Many that are One.* Not one person exists independently of everything else.

We could say that our perception of reality is sufficient to our purposes, but the status quo is a false, failed paradigm that cannot create a sustainable future. Basic education, sanitation, and health services could be provided to every person on the planet for what we instead choose to invest in military spending and recreational narcotics.

We may imagine that we are immune to the suffering that affects people in other countries, but the collective karma of cause-and-effect respects no national boundaries. What goes into the collective consciousness must play out through the collective consciousness. *What goes into the ecosystem stays in the ecosystem.*

A new script is being written within the collective consciousness as unrest grows over the top-down inequalities of the world's economic systems. It is written as the effects of climate change accelerate faster than previous projections. It is written as the spiritual evolution of mankind sweeps away the obsolete fundamentalism of guilt, punishment, and patriarchal domination. The form of this world is indeed "passing away." [15]

The *New Genesis* is collective Awareness. Collective Awareness evolves consciousness in the physical, by which we transform the physical nature of the universe so that the density of matter becomes wholly (holy) conscious.

Practice: *"The Common Good is My Good."*

The basis of collective Awareness may be summarized in one sentence: The Common Good is My Good.

What is the "Common Good"?

Some examples might include:

Clean air

Clean water

Universal healthcare

Universal higher education

Minimization of man-made pollution and waste

Personal freedom to become our best possible selves

Appreciation of the diversity of culture, ethnicity, and gender identity that enrich our societies

Resolution of societal and international conflicts without violence or coercion

Governments serve the best interests of their citizens

Non-participation and passive resistance become the highest expressions of opposition and dissent

Societies and nations recognize the necessity to contribute to the common good

Human beings become true stewards of the earth, for all of creation

As a "tree is known by the fruit it bears," our evolution of the Common Good will be known by our conscious choices to empower life, human life, and quality of life on this planet. [16]

Just for today, as we go about our daily activities, let us be mindful that, *"The Common Good is My Good."*

10. Earth Paradise

81. I am the storm, the wind, the rain
82. Fear nothing; embrace everything
83. This is Creation.
84. This is Life.

Why shouldn't the Earth be the best possible place it can be?

We come to the Earth to experience separation and to participate in the evolution of consciousness at this level of being. The unique challenge of our time in history is to facilitate the process of a great planetary renewal.

History has no claim on the possibilities of the present moment.

To begin, we don't need the right answers, so much as to ask the right questions, and to pursue the most empowering visions of all that we may become.

Why shouldn't the Earth be the best possible place it can be?

The Earth offers opportunities for survival, but no guarantees. There have always been challenges to our survival—starvation, cold, predators, drought, conflicts and wars. Millions of years ago, life for our hominid ancestors on the African savannah may have seemed simpler, but was it any less difficult?

We are the recipients of the evolutionary success of everyone who came before us. How many toiled at the earth, suffered, and fought that we might arrive at this moment in history? We owe no less to the generations that come after us.

Why shouldn't the Earth be the best possible place it can be?

The quality of life on this planet expands or contracts to the extent that we seek to improve it.

Our mission here is to influence the future.

Though what we do as individuals may seem to have little effect, even a small nudge can sometimes change the trajectory of a much larger object. Imagine what billions of small nudges might accomplish!

Why shouldn't the Earth be the best possible place it can be?

Our differences are a matter of information, not substance.

The injuries, grievances, and paradigms of the past no longer serve us. Today's "enemy" may be tomorrow's trading partner, friend, or family member.

The best thing we can do for our children and grandchildren is to *make our world the best possible place for everyone's children and grandchildren.*

85. Where One Heart is true
86. Others may follow

We say we want change, but we want someone else to do it for us.

We say we want change, but we don't want to leave the safety of our house, our routine, our fixed beliefs.

We say we want change, but it's easier to do the same thing we did yesterday, and somehow expect different results.

We build comfort zones around ourselves and fill them with familiar objects and routines. We use the same beverage cup, travel the same routes, go to the same stores, and surf the same websites. We run on automatic pilot because everything is the same. Our minds begin to turn off because we no longer have to adapt to changing circumstances or make new, conscious choices.

"Sameness" seemingly equals survival: If our current conditions support survival, and nothing changes, then it seems "only logical" that we shall continue to survive. For that reason, some aspect of ourselves wants today to be like yesterday, and wants tomorrow to be like today.

The problem is that the status quo may be a very miserable place. We may be "stuck" in an unhealthful relationship, job, or behavioral pattern. Nor does it understand that a failure to act now could create more serious issues later on; for example, if we neglect our health or fail to plan for the future.

Other people also unconsciously want things to stay the same. For that reason, they'll find ways to undermine the people around them—us—to ensure that nothing changes. That sabotage could be as subtle as a doubtful glance, or as overt as obstructive behavior. It's not that they are intentionally trying to do harm, but that they're reacting from that lower level of the brain that is mesmerized by stability.

Any experience capable of producing different results or teaching us something new is also by definition a challenging experience. If an activity does not make us uncomfortable, then it's just some version of the same things we've always done, and our lives remain the same.

True change always occurs against resistance. A sad fact is that those who resist progressive change are actually fighting against their own best interests, and against the best interests of their children and grandchildren.

The truth is, if people want to do something, they'll find a reason to do it. If they don't want to do something, they'll find an excuse not to do it. We think the justification creates the motivation, but it is just the opposite: Motivation precedes justification. For example, if a company says that they can't do something because "it's against the rules," what that means is that they didn't want to do it so they created the rules against it. But if an executive of that company wants to do the same thing, then those "rules" will be quietly ignored; and so it is within the artificial hierarchies of government—those in positions of power escape consequences that easily ensnare those of lesser rank.

A problem is not perceived to be a problem until the responsible parties—those who created it or those who could resolve it—experience the direct consequences of their actions or inactions. Until then, anyone complaining about the problem will be seen as "the problem." This is a classic, "kill the messenger" scenario.

Want to solve a problem? Then find a way to non-violently re-distribute the discomfort, the aggravation, and the inconvenience of the situation to the responsible parties.

The fact is, people—and nations—respect strength and exploit weakness. Whether it be freedom, democracy, or equality, that for which we do not insist will be taken from us.

The goal of achieving an Earth Paradise is not naive or impossible, but essential—essential to any reasonable quality of life for the life forms on this planet, and for the survival of our own species.

The problems we have are the challenges we came here to overcome. Every obstacle in our path is an opportunity to find a better way.

To change the world, we must consciously change what

we value. If we change what we value we change markets, and markets change the world.

We change markets by consciously making more healthful choices about what we consume—not only in our bodies, but in our homes, our communities, our environment, our entertainment and media choices, and how we daily choose to live our lives.

As conscious consumers, we can find better solutions, make better choices, and "vote" accordingly with our pocketbooks. We have the power to say, "No, I don't want that." Or, "No, I want something better." Or, "No, that doesn't work for me anymore." What we consume will increase, and what we reject will decrease.

One day at a time, each one of us, doing one small thing, has the power to change the world. *Where one heart is true, others may follow, and that becomes a movement.*

How are some ways that change can occur?

Change occurs when we keep pushing for change to happen.

Change occurs when one party is more persistent than the other.

Change occurs when the arguments for change become more convincing than the arguments against change.

Change occurs when opposing parties agree on mutually beneficial compromises.

Change occurs when we overcome the inertia of the status quo.

Change occurs when the pain of maintaining current conditions becomes greater than the pain of breaking free.

Change occurs when the threat of loss overrides the comfort of staying the same.

Change occurs when it becomes the commonly accepted truth.

Change occurs when it becomes a necessity for survival.

Change occurs when it becomes the path of least resistance.

Change occurs when it becomes the best product for the best price.

Change occurs when it becomes an object of envy for those who do not have it.

Change occurs when we become more aware of the consequences of our thoughts and deeds.

Change occurs when we act from a higher state of being.

And for some, change will only occur when it best serves their limited self-interest and greed.

87. Now is the time to redeem all that has become before.

Practice: *The Last Question*

"God" is not somewhere else, but HERE, NOW, EVERYWHERE, as EVERYTHING.

"Truth" is not an intellectual understanding, but a state of Being.

No one is better than anyone else, no one is less.

There is only one boat and we are all in it.

What you do affects me, and what I do affects you.

There is no "other" to attack, save for the illusions of our own minds.

We don't need a riot in the streets, we need a riot in our hearts.

We are the revolution we seek, a revolution within consciousness.

Why shouldn't the Earth be the best possible place it can be?

It can be and it will be, because that is what we do and why we are here.

Individually and collectively, our legacy grows each day with how we choose to live our lives.

Let go of the past, live in the now, and act from a higher state of being.

By our conscious choices, let us dedicate ourselves to planetary renewal and service. Let us empower *life, human life,* and *quality of life* on this planet.

At the end of the day, and the end of our lives, a last question remains:

Was the world a better place that we were in it?

Living The Gospel of One

A Thirty-Day Guide

All hearts rise to the new paradigm
Old Earth shall be no more

Day 1: Essay 1

Read Essay 1, "In the Beginning"

In today's reading, was there a verse, a sentence, or an idea that particularly resonated with you? If so, write it on a note and place it somewhere it can be seen during your daily activities (for example, on your mirror, the dash of your vehicle, or your computer monitor or screen).

Questions for Review:

What was the One Thought that began creation?

What is the story that the universe wants to tell?

How do we evolve?

What purpose do challenges to our survival or to our well-being serve?

Practice:

As we encounter the people and situations that manifest in our experiences throughout the day, make a conscious effort to remember that no matter the circumstances, "Everything plays a part in the Evolution of Consciousness."

Day 2: Essay 1

Read or review Essay 1, "In the Beginning"

Recite Verses 1-14 aloud or silently.

Questions for Review:

In reference to Verse 12, how might "truth lead to error"? Hint: Sometimes we are never more dangerous than when we think we have "THE ANSWER" or the only perception of what is true. Can you give an example of this bias in your own thinking or behavior?

Practice:

As we encounter the people and situations that manifest in our experiences throughout the day, make a conscious effort to remember that no matter the circumstances, "Everything plays a part in the Evolution of Consciousness."

Day 3: Essay 1

Read or review Essay 1, "In the Beginning"

Recite Verses 1-14 aloud or silently.

Questions for Review:
What do the struggles and efforts of human experience serve to accomplish?

Practice:
As circumstances allow during the day, notice the personalities that are disagreeable to you in some way. These could be family members, friends, co-workers, politicians, or random people on the street. In each case, apply the idea that, "Everything plays a part in the Evolution of Consciousness."

Day 4: Essay 2

Read Essay 2, "From Wholeness"

In today's reading, was there a verse, a sentence, or an idea that particularly resonated with you? If so, write it on a note and place it somewhere it can be seen during your daily activities.

Meditate:

Meditate using the instructions in Essay 2, "A Simple Meditation," or the meditation methodology of your choice.

If you are new to meditation, be mindful that the measure of success is not how long or how deeply you meditate, but how consistently you practice. Forming the habit is more important than the quantity or quality of the practice.

Questions for Review:

Where do all paths lead?

Practice:

With your hand placed over your upper chest, ask yourself, "Where might the peace of God be found?" While taking several deep breaths, silently or aloud verbalize the answer: "Right here, right now" (i.e., in the present Awareness).

Day 5: Essay 2

Read or review Essay 2, "From Wholeness"

Recite Verses 15-18 aloud or silently.

Meditate.

Questions for Review:
Who are we, really?

Practice:
With your hand placed over your upper chest, ask yourself, "Where might the peace of God be found?" While taking several deep breaths, silently or aloud verbalize the answer: "Right here, right now" (i.e., in the present Awareness).

Day 6: Essay 2

Read or review Essay 2, "From Wholeness"

Recite Verses 15-18 aloud or silently.

Meditate.

Questions for Review:
Where is all the madness in the world?
What is meditation?

Practice:
With your hand placed over your upper chest, ask yourself, "Where might the peace of God be found?" While taking several deep breaths, silently or aloud verbalize the answer: "Right here, right now" (i.e., in the present Awareness).

Day 7: Essay 3

Read Essay 3, "Source"

In today's reading, was there a verse, a sentence, or an idea that particularly resonated with you? If so, write it on a note and place it somewhere it can be seen during your daily activities.

Meditate.

Review:
What is the *Godself*?
What is "separation" and what is its purpose?

Practice:
Today, as you encounter other people, no matter who they are, their apparent station in life, or how they behave, remember that, "No one is better than anyone else. No one is less."

Day 8: Essay 3

Read or review essay 3, "Source"

Recite Verses 19-24 aloud or silently.

Meditate.

Review:
What is the resolution we seek?

Practice:
Today, as you encounter other people, no matter who they are, their apparent station in life, or how they behave, remember that, "No one is better than anyone else. No one is less."

Day 9: Essay 3

Read or review essay 3, "Source"

Recite Verses 19-24 aloud or silently.

Meditate.

Questions for Review:
What are rank and status?
Who is better than anyone else? Who is less?

Practice:
Today, as you encounter other people, no matter who they are, their apparent station in life, or how they behave, remember that, "No one is better than anyone else. No one is less."

Day 10: Essay 4

Read essay 4, "My Beloved"

In today's reading, was there a verse, a sentence, or an idea that particularly resonated with you? If so, write it on a note and place it somewhere it can be seen during your daily activities.

Meditate

Review:
What is Source?
What are the four basic misunderstandings about the nature of God and Man?

Practice:
Practice non-judgment. As soon as we become aware that we have been triggered by someone or some situation, remember that, "I do not need to judge this."

Day 11: Essay 4

Read or review Essay 4, "My Beloved"

Recite Verses 25-38 aloud or silently.

Meditate

Questions for Review:
What is the "Fall of Man"?
Everywhere we look, what does *Godself* see?
Who judges us?

Practice:
Practice non-judgment. As soon as we become aware that we have been triggered by someone or some situation, remember that, "I do not need to judge this."

Day 12: Essay 4

Read or review Essay 4, "My Beloved"

Recite Verses 25-38 aloud or silently.

Meditate

Questions for Review:
What must play out through the collective consciousness?
How are we alike?
What might be revealed by the worst behavior among us?
What are projections of criticism, blame, and guilt?

Practice:
Practice non-judgment. As soon as we become aware that we
have been triggered by someone or some situation, remember
that, "I do not need to judge this."

Day 13: Essay 5

Read essay 5, "To Change the World"

In today's reading, was there a verse, a sentence, or an idea that particularly resonated with you? If so, write it on a note and place it somewhere it can be seen during your daily activities.

Meditate

Questions for Review:
What is the basis of aggression?
What is underlying basis of all that is perceived to be wrong in the world?

Practice:
To change the world for the better, practice kindness. Right now, today, practice kindness in whatever form or opportunities express themselves to you. Note that even simple things add up and contribute to the overall good.

Day 14: Essay 5

Read or review Essay 5, "To Change the World"

Recite verses 39-46 aloud or silently.

Meditate

Review:
What is karma?
When does karmic justice begin?

Practice:
To change the world for the better, practice kindness. Right now, today, practice kindness in whatever form or opportunities express themselves to you. Note that even simple things add up and contribute to the overall good.

Day 15: Essay 5

Read or review Essay 5, "To Change the World"

Recite verses 39-46 aloud or silently.

Meditate

Review:
How could we change the world for the better in a single day?
What is the essential nature of "doing the right thing"?

Practice:
To change the world for the better, practice kindness. Right now, today, practice kindness in whatever form or opportunities express themselves to you. Note that even simple things add up and contribute to the overall good.

Day 16: Essay 6

Read Essay 6, "Clearing Karma"

In today's reading, was there a verse, a sentence, or an idea that particularly resonated with you? If so, write it on a note and place it somewhere it can be seen during your daily activities.

Meditate.

Questions for Review:
Why do people do bad things?
What are the characteristics of low states of Awareness?

Practice:
Forgive the unpleasant situations or personalities you encounter, and forgive your response to those events.
If it's helpful, use the three-step forgiveness method:
1. Forgive the other person or situation.
2. Forgive yourself for whatever label you projected onto the other person or the situation.
3. Forgive your lack of patience with the other person or situation.

Day 17: Essay 6

Read or review Essay 6, "Clearing Karma"

Recite verses 47-49 aloud or silently.

Meditate.

Questions for Review:
When bad things happen, what are three things we might consider in response?

Practice:
Forgive the unpleasant situations or personalities you encounter, and forgive your response to those events.

If it's helpful, use the three-step forgiveness method:

1. Forgive the other person or situation.

2. Forgive yourself for whatever label you projected onto the other person or the situation.

3. Forgive your lack of patience with the other person or situation.

Day 18: Essay 6

Read or review Essay 6, "Clearing Karma"

Recite verses 47-49 aloud or silently.

Meditate.

Questions for Review:
What is forgiveness?
Is the universe a grand morality play of "good" versus "evil"?
If not, what is it?

Practice:
Forgive the unpleasant situations or personalities you encounter, and forgive your response to those events.
If it's helpful, use the three-step forgiveness method:
1. Forgive the other person or situation.
2. Forgive yourself for whatever label you projected onto the other person or the situation.
3. Forgive your lack of patience with the other person or situation.

Day 19: Essay 7

Read Essay 7, "As You Love One Another"

In today's reading, was there a verse, a sentence, or an idea that particularly resonated with you? If so, write it on a note and place it somewhere it can be seen during your daily activities.

Meditate.

Questions for Review:
What is "separation"?

Practice:
During the day, aloud or silently, unconditionally declare "I love you" to at least five objects of your perception. These could be people, animals, plants, or inanimate objects.
For additional ways to practice love, see the "Practicing Love" pages in the Addendums.

Day 20: Essay 7

Read or review Essay 7, "As You Love One Another"

Recite verses 50-58 aloud or silently.

Meditate.

Questions for Review:
What is the basis for who we think we are?
What is the dream state?

Practice:
During the day, aloud or silently, unconditionally declare "I love you" to at least five objects of your perception. These could be people, animals, plants, or inanimate objects.
For additional ways to practice love, see the "Practicing Love" pages in the Addendums.

Day 21: Essay 7

Read or review Essay 7, "As You Love One Another"

Recite verses 50-58 aloud or silently.

Meditate.

Questions for Review:
What must we do to experience Wholeness?
What must we do to fully love one another?

Practice:
During the day, aloud or silently, unconditionally declare "I love you" to at least five objects of your perception. These could be people, animals, plants, or inanimate objects.
For additional ways to practice love, see the "Practicing Love" pages in the Addendums.

Day 22: Essay 8

Read Essay 8, "Compassion"

In today's reading, was there a verse, a sentence, or an idea that particularly resonated with you? If so, write it on a note and place it somewhere it can be seen during your daily activities.

Meditate.

Questions for Review:
What are the failed paradigms of consensual reality?

Practice:
Today, practice compassion. Be courteous. Be kind. Be respectful. And as opportunities to help present themselves, however small they may seem, follow through.

Day 23: Essay 8

Read or review Essay 8, "Compassion"

Recite verses 59-72 aloud or silently.

Meditate.

Questions for Review:
What are three ways we might help facilitate a revolution of consciousness?

Practice:
Today, practice compassion. Be courteous. Be kind. Be respectful. And as opportunities to help present themselves, however small they may seem, follow through.

Day 24: Essay 8

Read or review Essay 8, "Compassion"

Recite verses 59-72 aloud or silently.

Meditate.

Questions for Review:
Where is our power to obtain better results?

Practice:
Today, practice compassion. Be courteous. Be kind. Be respectful. And as opportunities to help present themselves, however small they may seem, follow through.

Day 25: Essay 9

Read Essay 9, "Adam and Eve"

In today's reading, was there a verse, a sentence, or an idea that particularly resonated with you? If so, write it on a note and place it somewhere it can be seen during your daily activities.

Meditate.

Questions for Review:
How do we treat our fellow creatures and the Earth?

Practice:
As we go about our daily activities, be mindful that, "The Common Good is My Good."

Day 26: Essay 9

Read or review Essay 9, "Adam and Eve"

Recite verses 73-80 aloud or silently.

Meditate.

Questions for Review:

What is the new script that is being written?

What is the New Genesis?

Practice:

As we go about our daily activities, be mindful that, "The Common Good is My Good."

Day 27: Essay 9

Read or review Essay 9, "Adam and Eve"

Recite verses 73-80 aloud or silently.

Meditate.

Questions for Review:
What are some examples of the Common Good?

Practice:
As we go about our daily activities, be mindful that, "The Common Good is My Good."

Day 28: Essay 10

Read Essay 10, "Earth Paradise"

In today's reading, was there a verse, a sentence, or an idea that particularly resonated with you? If so, write it on a note and place it somewhere it can be seen during your daily activities.

Meditate.

Questions for Review:

What might today's "enemy" be tomorrow?

What is the best thing we can do for our children and grandchildren?

Practice:

Do something today, however small, that makes the world a better place because you are in it.

Day 29: Essay 10

Read or review Essay 10, "Earth Paradise"

Recite verses 81-87 aloud or silently.

Meditate.

Questions for Review:
What are some of the ways that people—including ourselves—resist or sabotage change?

Practice:
Do something today, however small, that makes the world a better place because you are in it.

Day 30: Essay 10

Read or review Essay 10, "Earth Paradise"

Recite verses 81-87 aloud or silently.

Meditate.

Questions for Review:
How does change occur?

Practice:
Do something today, however small, that makes the world a better place because you are in it.

Day 31 and Beyond: The Three Essentials

Read "The Three Essentials" in the Addendums section.

Several times a day, take one or more deep breaths and fully exhale each time to allow the body to relax. With one or both hands, touch the tips of the thumb, ring, and middle fingers together, allowing the index and small fingers to relax. Then recite verses 88-90. One by one, feel or imagine your full coherence with each verse (for example, what would it feel like to truly "Forgive Everything"? If you can't feel it, then to the best of your ability, imagine what that feeling might be like.)

Author's note: Touching the three fingertips together acts as a physical "anchor" to bring the three verses into a tactile union. Practiced consistently, touching the fingertips together becomes a cue to for the body to relax into the feelings of forgiveness, love, and trust. You could also begin your daily meditations by practicing this technique.

Read "Practicing Love"
On a daily basis, implement at least one of the practices.

Review the Essays
From time to time, open the book and read whatever presents itself.

I am the storm, the wind, the rain
Fear nothing, embrace everything
This is Creation
This is Life.

Addendums

Everywhere I look
I see Me.
With every breath
I am this.

The Three Essentials

88. Forgive Everything
89. Love All
90. Trust Creation

Forgive Everything. Forgiveness helps to clear discordant energy from both individual and collective consciousness. Thinking of our own errors, if we had known better, we would have done better. And so it is with our fellow beings—if they were truly conscious, they would have also done better. Life, it's messy.

Love All. The universe is the manifest body of the divine. To love All is to love God.

Trust Creation. The universe will reach its perfect fulfillment no matter what we do. If a billion civilizations rise and fall on billions of planets, the evolution of consciousness will progress because of it, not in spite of it. Why? Because that is what the universe does. It evolves greater and greater levels of consciousness.

We may not know exactly how we are going to get there, but we can be confident in its eventual outcome. Regardless of whether it occurs right here, right now, or hundreds or thousands of years into the future, "The universe knows what it is doing, the *Godself* is not amiss, We are the light That creates the heavens, The love that guides the stars" (verses 50-54).

Practicing Love

From Essay 6 "As You Love One Another":

To love one another we must fully love ourselves, love the earth, love all of the organisms and creatures that give life to this planet; love the sun, the moon, and the stars in the sky. To love everyone and everything is the true meaning of, "Love God with all your spirit, all your heart, and all your mind."

Just for today, pause at random moments throughout the day to unconditionally express, "I love you," to at least five things. Repeat the "I love you" statement three times to each of the objects of perception. These could be people, animals, plants, or inanimate objects in the environment. To start, we might place one palm over our upper chest, and declare, "I love you" three times to ourselves!

It doesn't matter what the object is, because as the manifest body of the divine, the universe is God everywhere in all things at all times, and truly, "Everywhere I look, I see Me."

Our intention forms a loving connection to the objects of our perception. With continued practice, we come to love everyone and everything. Effectively, as incarnate beings we become Love.

Additional Suggestions for Practicing Love:

Send love to the objects of sensation and perception without labeling or judging them in any way. For example, to send love to a tree outside your window, express "I love you" to the tree without the need to identify it as a tree.

What do you see? Send love to those experiences of visual perception.

What do you hear? Send love to those experiences of audio perception.

What do you smell? Send love to those experiences of scent perception.

What do you taste? Send love to those experiences of taste perception.

What do you feel? Send love to those bodily experiences, regardless of whether they are perceptions of touch or feelings within the body. Do you feel your body's contact with the chair or floor on which you sit? Send love to that sensation. Do you feel your feet in contact with the ground or floor? Send love to that sensation.

When your heart swells with inspiration, or aches with sadness, send love to those sensations.

What thoughts are you experiencing? Send love to those thoughts.

NOTE: Just as we can love someone without liking what they do, the same can be said for our other experiences. The point of these practices is to love everything unconditionally regardless of how it manifests in our awareness.

The Love Challenges:

Each day of the week, take one of the aforementioned sensory or perceptual suggestions, and practice that throughout the day. For example, one day focus on sending love to everything you see; the next day, focus on sending love to everything you hear; and so on.

At least one day a week, throughout the day, no matter who it is or what is happening, unconditionally project love to everyone and everything.

Practicing Gratitude

The more we direct our attention on a thing, the more it increases in our awareness. For example, imagine yourself watching vehicles pass by on a busy highway. You decide to count the number of blue cars you see. After a length of time, you have counted quite a number of blue cars. Now ask yourself, how many red cars did you see? You probably don't know, because that wasn't your focus.

And so it is with gratitude, or anything else for that matter. The more things that you express gratitude for, the more things for which to be grateful come to mind.

Practicing gratitude serves as a counter-balance to "negativity bias," the brain's tendency to focus on negative thoughts and events. That bias could be seen as a survival mechanism to alert us to potential "threats" in our environment, but the sheer number of problems and stresses we encounter in the modern world far exceed the physical threats our ancestors faced eons ago. Unchecked, "negativity bias" can dominate too much of our time and attention.

The Five Gratitudes: "I am grateful for..."

At the end of the day, as you drift off to sleep, express gratitude for at least five things that happened during the day. If you initially can't think of anything, or if the day was unusually difficult, begin by expressing gratitude that the day is over with. You could also begin by expressing gratitude that you have a roof over your head, a bed to sleep in, a pillow to rest your head, and so on with other simple things.

Why five? A minimum of five expressions of gratitude stimulates more thoughts of things to be grateful for. The ideas do not have to be anything grand. Typically, you may drift off to sleep thinking of more and more things for which to be grateful.

TIP: To begin the practice, write a numeral "5" on a piece of paper and place it on your pillow or somewhere it can be seen as you retire for the evening.

The Gratitude Challenge:

At least one day a week, throughout the day, no matter the situation or personalities, unconditionally project gratitude to everyone and everything.

A Simple Meditation

Meditation is the art of waking up from the world of our imaginations and beliefs. The key to learning meditation is to 1) keep it simple and 2) begin.

As with anything new, this may feel awkward at first but becomes easier with practice.

NOTE: This method uses nasal breathing for both inhalations and exhalations. Other methods emphasize breathing in through the nose and out through the mouth. Do whichever works best for you.

Start your timer if you are using one.

Sit upright in a chair with your feet on the floor, or in any position that supports good posture.

To begin, sit relaxed. Place one open palm high across your upper chest (just below the suprasternal notch between the shoulder blades), and inhale deeply through your nose. Feel the expansion of your chest and your lower belly as you inhale. Hold the breath for a few seconds and then exhale slowly and fully through the nose, allowing your shoulders to sink into a more relaxed pose. Repeat for a total of three inhalations and exhalations.

Now sit erect with good posture. Lower your chin a bit so that the neck muscles relax. Place your hands in your lap, the back of one hand resting in the palm of the other, or alternatively rest the hands on the thighs, palms up for receptivity, or palms down for grounding.

Close your eyes.

Breathe in and out through your nose, with the mouth lightly closed (the jaws should be relaxed, not clenched). NOTE: There are several advantages to nasal breathing, among which is an increase in the production of nitric oxide, which dilates blood vessels and thereby lowers blood pressure and increases oxygenation.

Sit quietly. With relaxed focus, follow the rhythm of your breath. Focus on the in-and-out flow of air through your nostrils, or the slight rise and fall of your chest, or the gentle expansion and relaxation of your lower belly. The point is to focus on the present moment, whatever it may be. This is about flow, not force.

Without strain, slow your breathing so that the time between respirations is gradually extended.

Thoughts will come. Do not judge or criticize yourself. The mind generates thoughts simply because that is what it does. As soon as you become aware that you are thinking, simply return focus to your breath. This cycle may repeat dozens or even hundreds of times depending on the length of the meditation. Any awareness of the resumption of thoughts is an indication of progress, not failure.

As thoughts arise, it may be helpful to once again place an open palm high across your upper chest, breathing slowly and deeply several times. Feel the air as it expands your thoracic cavity from the lungs all the way down to the lower abdomen. Exhale slowly and fully. Maintain the posture and repeat as long as needed to help calm the mind.

If especially discordant thoughts intrude, open your eyes and look straight ahead. While keeping your head stationary and your eyes on the same horizontal plane, move your eyes back-and-forth from extreme left to extreme right, without strain. Resume meditation as the thoughts recede.

With practice, the interval between thoughts will lengthen. These seemingly empty spaces or gaps become experiences of profound peace.

When the timer sounds, turn it off. Rest quietly for a short while, or return to meditation if you wish.

If you feel at all "spacey" or ungrounded when you rise, walk around and lightly stomp your feet a few times.

Twelve Paradigms

Pick a paradigm as a "thought for the day." Notice how that thought might manifest itself in your experiences throughout the day.

We are all here to experience life as human beings.

We are all here to evolve consciousness.

All paths lead to *Here and Now*.

All hierarchies are contrived. *No one is better than anyone else, no one is less.*

Unhelpful projections of criticism, blame, and guilt are a form of personal and collective self-harm.

To change the world, *practice kindness.*

Forgiveness clears discordant karma.

To love God, *love God as everyone and everything.*

There is only *one* boat and we are all in it.

The Common Good is my good.

If we change what we value, we change markets, and *markets change the world.*

Where one heart is true, others may follow.

Scriptural References

Scriptures referenced or paraphrased in the text:

[1] "...the Kingdom of God is within you" – Luke 17:21

[2] "...unless a man be born again [born into a new awareness], he cannot see the Kingdom of God" – John 3:3

[3] "...This is the pearl of such exquisite quality that the gem dealer sold everything he had to obtain it" – Matthew 13:45-46

[4] "Experience the peace of God that defies understanding" – Philippians 4:5-7

[5] "I and my Father are One" - John 10:30

[6] "Judge not that you be not judged: for as you judge, so shall you be judged" – Matthew 7:12

[7] "As you sow, so shall you reap" – Galatians 6:7

[8] "Do unto others as you would have them do unto you" - Matthew 7:12

[9] "Love your neighbor as yourself" – Mark 12:31

[10] "Forgive them, Father, for they know not what they do" - Luke 23:34

[11] "What you forgive on earth (individuated consciousness) will be forgiven in heaven (the collective consciousness)" – John 20:23

[12] "Love God with all your spirit, all your heart, and all your mind" – Matthew 22:37

[13] "Let the dead bury the dead" – Luke 9:60

[14] "...made in God's own image" – Genesis 1:27

[15] The form of this world is indeed "passing away" – Corinthians 7:31

[16] "A tree is known by the fruit it bears" – Luke 6:44

Glossary

Awakening - The experience of unfiltered Awareness, free of the illusions created by mind

Awareness – What we truly are

Bliss - Unfiltered Awareness

Egoic - Pertaining to ego

Fall of Man - An erroneous judgment applied to the illusion of separation within the survival mechanisms of mind

Forgiveness - The art of clearing discordant energy from the collective consciousness

Fundamentalism - A misguided projection of patriarchal domination, guilt, and punishment

Godself - The manifest body of the Divine expressed as the indivisible totality of all things; Source ("the One") experiencing Self as The Many; the sum total of all manifest experiences within consciousness

Identity - An assemblage of perceptions, understandings, and memories accumulated over time (essentially, a pattern of belief)

Incarnation - Individuated experiences projected from Source

Karma – A neutral feedback mechanism within consciousness; the answer to the question, "If I do this, what happens?"; the simultaneous flow of cause-and-effect; a living, dynamic composition that plays out across time and circumstance

Meditation – The art of waking up from the world of our imaginations and beliefs

New Genesis - Collective Awareness; "We" not "me"; "unity consciousness"

Original Sin - An erroneous concept applied to the perception of contrasts within Awareness

Separation – The illusion created by mind that we are separate from one another, apart from the world we inhabit, and apart from Source; a story we tell ourselves to facilitate the experience of the Many among the One

Source - Indivisible Unity; the origin of everything; "No-thing-ness"

Questions for the Author

Q1: What inspired you to write, "The Gospel of One"?

A1: From an early age, I struggled to understand what is going on in this world. The things that people did made no sense to me. For the longest time, I wondered what was wrong with people, and then at some point I came to an understanding that there is quite a variation in the way that people are "wired." In the scheme of things, my personality "type" or temperament is in the minority, and the "types" of other people are more within the "normal" range (there is no good or bad there, but simply a worthwhile distinction).

Q2: By what authority did you write, "The Gospel of One"?

A2: None. By formal education, I am not a theologian. I am not a guru. I am not a scholar. I am not a saint. I am not an evangelist. If a label must be applied, then "accidental theologian" seems apt.

Q3: What is your religious background?

A3: As explained in the Preface, I was raised in a fundamentalist Christian tradition, but its "fire-and-brimstone" messaging of, "God loves you, but you'll never be good enough, so you're going to burn in hell forever," wasn't congruent with the higher ideas I read in the Gospels.

Q4: Do you consider yourself a Christian?

A4: If being a Christian is defined by traditional Christian theology and what we see of the "evangelical" church of the early 21st century, then the answer is ABSOLUTELY NOT!

I suspect the historical Yeshua ("Jesus") was more like Buddha, who preceded him by several hundred years. That is to say, Yeshua was a man who had "awakening" experiences, either through meditation, asceticism, mysticism, or the ingestion of psychotropic plants, all of which he may have practiced during his "40 days in the desert." I think all those practices were purged from Yeshua's teachings by the religious patriarchy who saw more power and control in selling salvation than in what Yeshua actually taught.

Q5: Were the "The Verses" in "The Gospel of One" channeled?

A5: In my own mind, "The Verses" are a mix of revelation and inspiration received during a time in which I did a lot of meditation. Some came through quite strongly, others less so. I would love to say that "spirit guides," "ascended masters," or other such entities appeared before me and told me what to write, but in my own experience I can only speculate that "The Verses" originated from a more expansive state of

Awareness—what we truly are rather what we imagine ourselves to be in this limited human experience.

Q6: Aren't you just "cherry picking" scripture to advance your own views?

A6: Yes, but dramatically less so than the "cherry picking" of the early "leaders" of the church who suppressed teachings that did not agree with the "salvation" agenda they wanted to push on the masses. The gnostic Gospel of Thomas is a prime example of that suppression.

Q7: In Essay 2, "From Wholeness," you write: "The pursuit of 'Enlightenment' can become a false paradigm..." Can you say more about that?

A7: "Enlightenment" is the western translation of a Buddhist term which more closely means "awakening" or "to wake up." In my limited but direct experience of expanded Awareness, "Awakening" is a more accurate term, as the experience is truly like "waking up" from the illusions of mind. In my view, "Enlightenment" suggests we should become something different than what we are, whereas—for those who wish to pursue it—it is more a process of waking up from everything we are not. As the text says, "...we are already that which we seek."

Harking back to the time when I did a lot of meditation, I had two short-lived experiences of "Awakening" in which all the illusions created by mind fell away. I was not transported to some alternate dimension—the room was still the room, but without all the labels, values, and models of separation as projected by mind. In that state of unfiltered Awareness, there were no "things," just Awareness itself.

It was BLISS, like something you can't even imagine, a state you would never want to leave. Perhaps paradoxically, my individuated Awareness laughed hysterically at the notion that I could have ever believed anything I'd ever thought was true. And then after what was probably no more than ten minutes in what seemed like heaven--"right here, right now, and a place we never left" as it says in Essay 2--I screamed "No!" in horror when I felt my mind re-constructing "normal" consensual reality.

I think these experiences were an act of Grace, to show me What Is. They were short-lived because that is not what I am here for. As you, I am here to experience what it is to be a human being, and to participate in the evolution of consciousness through our collective experiences on this planet. For that reason, in my view, you don't have to pursue Awakening, Enlightenment, Salvation, or whatever. It's equally okay to simply live your life, to just be a decent human being, without any of that. It's whatever your individuated Awareness is called to do.

Q8: In Essay 4, you refer to God as "She." Are you saying that God is a woman?

A8: The use of "She" simply felt correct. The divine feminine has been celebrated in many ways by many names in cultures and spiritual practices around the world. Indeed, in a thousand-year-old Hindu text, the creative force that generates the universe is identified as female: "Through Her own Will, Awareness unfolds the universe that is the 'canvas' that is Herself" [Christopher Wallis. The Recognition Sutras. Boulder, Colorado, Mattamayūra Press, 2017.].

Unfortunately, the idea of God as "He," or "Our Father in Heaven" carries a lot of projections of patriarchal supremacy, guilt, and punishment.

Who can deny that the male energy that dominates our world—specifically, the quest for acquisition, power, and control—is responsible for most of humanity's woes?

Why not flip that on its head and empower a new, more beneficial paradigm?

Why not put an end to this, "Father knows best and everyone else can shut up" nonsense?

Why not think of God as a more nurturing, life-giving, motherly presence?

Whether we think of God as "The Mother, "The Father," or having no gender identification whatsoever, it's all just a manner of thinking. But that thinking does have consequences.

Perhaps better questions to ask are:

"What is more skillful?"

"Which paradigm better empowers *life, human life,* and *quality of life*?"

"How may we achieve a more helpful—and a more healthful—balance of female and male energies on this planet?"

In regards to the latter question, it seems the pendulum has swung so far in the direction of patriarchal domination that any semblance of the "middle" would still skew the balance in favor of toxic masculinity. Perhaps it is time for that pendulum to swing far, far in the opposite direction for a while?

Q9: In Essay 4, you also talk about "obsolete projections of patriarchal domination, guilt, and punishment." This seems to be aimed at fundamentalist theology. Do you have more to say about that?

A9: In my mind, fundamentalist theology is all about asserting power and control, especially in regards to women. From an anthropological point of view, it seems that the suppression of women seen in fundamentalist ideologies is all about controlling reproductive access to the females of the populace, even if those who do the controlling—thinking of elderly clerics—have no interest in propagating their own DNA. If true, then the subjugation of women in fundamentalist societies is not "holiness," it's *biology*; it's not divine will, it's *patriarchy*; it's not righteousness, it's *tyranny*.

What is the solution for those ensnared by fundamentalist ideologies? Verses 11~14 may offer a strategy:

> *11. As error may lead to truth*
> *12. And truth may lead to error*
> *13. Discern that which has value*
> *14. From that which does not.*

As a "tree is known by the fruit it bears" [16], does the teaching or belief respect individual sovereignty, self-expression, and equality? Or is it an obsolete projection of patriarchal domination, guilt, and punishment?

Q10: What are the influences that affected your spiritual evolution?

A10: There have been many, but as explained in the Preface, as a youngster the high ideas espoused by Yeshua (Jesus) in the canonical Gospels were formative, even though there was a disconnect between what I read in the scriptures compared to the projections of patriarchal guilt and punishment I heard coming from the pastor's pulpit.

One of the most transformative influences occurred when I was a young man and read Swami Prabhavananda and Christopher Isherwood's magnificent 1954 translation of the "Bhagavad-Gita: The Song of God," particularly Chapter 2, "The Yoga of Knowledge," wherein Krishna explains the eternal nature of what we are: "There never was a time when I did not exist, nor you, nor any of these kings. Nor is there any future in which we shall cease to be" [Swami Prabhavananda and Christopher Isherwood. Bhagavad-Gita: The Song of God. New York, New York, Mentor Books, 1954.].

Ram Dass's "Be Here Now" was also an early influence [Ram Dass. Be Here Now. San Cristobal, New Mexico. Lama Foundation, 1971.].

I treasured the first four books written by Carlos Castaneda. Although Castaneda's accounts of his alleged apprenticeship with a Yaqui sorcerer ("man of knowledge") have been categorized as fiction, that doesn't mean that they don't have something of value to say: "In my own life I could say I have traversed long, long paths, but I am not anywhere. Does this path have a heart? ...If it does, the path is good; if it doesn't, it is of no use." [Carlos Castaneda. The Teachings of Don Juan: A Yaqui Way of Knowledge. New York, New York. Simon and Schuster, 1968.]

Of course, no spiritual odyssey would be complete without Yogananda's 1946 classic, "Autobiography of a Yogi." [Paramahansa Yogananda. Autobiography of a Yogi. Self-Realization Fellowship, 1946, 2010.]

I generally agree with what I understand about Buddhism and yogic philosophy, but do not feel compelled to practice either. I think we each have to find our own way. If we don't experience it ourselves, then it's just mindless regurgitation of someone else's dogma. As Thoreau wrote in

"Walden," "What old people say you cannot do, you try and find that you can. Old deeds for old people, and new deeds for new" [Henry David Thoreau. Walden; or Life in the Woods. Boston, Massachusetts. Ticknor and Fields, 1854.]. Also—as previously stated—I think it's okay to just be a decent human being and live your life. That is sufficient. Even if you have an Awakening experience, you still have to live your life, or as Ram Dass wrote in "Be Here Now," you still need to "know your zip code" (i.e, address). If you are called to do more, then that's fine, too.

I would probably be only half as "attuned" to spiritual matters if not for the Reiki training I received from a wonderful teacher years ago (that's a Reiki joke, for those who are familiar with how Reiki is taught). Reiki opened the door to a world of metaphysical experiences, from the subtle to the startling. For example, as I was providing a Reiki session for a client from a cancer support group, I kept seeing flashes of men in black shirts with white collars. I asked her about it at the end of the session. She said that her late husband had been a priest who left the clergy to marry her, something she had never revealed in previous sessions. There have been "glitch in the matrix" moments when my visual perception of a scene distorts into something like an early analog television set with its horizontal control out of adjustment, before normal perception snapped back into place. The sense of those experiences was that my normal perception of reality is a projected illusion. All that said, I caution the reader not to get caught up in the pursuit of the "woo-woo" aspects of metaphysical experiences. As with meditation, such things are a matter of flow, not force.

In regards to "energy work" modalities (Reiki, healing touch, etc.), Brugh Joy's book, "Joy's Way" was also an informative resource [W. Brugh Joy, M.D.. Joy's Way: A Map for the Transformational Journey. New York, New York. Jeremy P. Tarcher/Putnam, 1979.].

The writings of Adyashanti resonate with me quite strongly: "I laughed, because I realized that what I was searching for was always right here, that the enlightenment for which I was seeking was literally the space that I existed in." [Adyashanti. Falling Into Grace. Boulder, Colorado. Sounds True, Inc., 2011, 2013.]

The teachings of the paqos (holy (wo)men) of the high Andes in Peru, particularly their veneration of "Pacha Mama" (our Earth Mother), have also been influential: "Dear Mother Earth... May the Light occupy this world as we help to open the Way, so that all are blessed, unified and inclined to a loving path..." [Wium, Jeffrey. Wisdomkeepers, Paqo Andino. Wiumworks Media, 2015. 1 hr, 28 min.]

More recently, Christopher M. Bache's book, "LSD and the Mind of the Universe - Diamonds from Heaven" has been transformative due to his vivid descriptions of the detoxification and healing of the collective consciousness [Christopher M. Bache, PhD.. LSD and the Mind of the Universe - Diamonds from Heaven. Rochester, Vermont. Park

Street Press, 2019.].

Overall, I've had exposure to many metaphysical influences, too numerous to name here.

Q11: The introductory verses [verses 59-68] of Essay 8, "Compassion" seem apocalyptic. What more can you say about that?

A11: These verses came through very clearly, but I have no specific information about said cataclysmic event. I can only speculate that if, and when it occurs, we'll know it. I also believe that the future is at least as much a matter of possibilities as probabilities, depending on the changes that occur in the interim.

Q12: Will there be a sequel to "The Gospel of One"?

A12: The genesis of "The Gospel of One" was a paper I wrote for a psychology class in 2003. Therefore, at this point "The Gospel of One" has been gestating for more than twenty years, and the form it takes here has been a journey of more than a decade. All of which is to say that if the universe wants me to write a direct sequel, it better "step on the gas" (i.e., accelerate the process).

Q13: What do you see as the future of mankind?

A13: Years ago, I had a vision that each individuated human consciousness would evolve to become a pillar of light, so that billions of pillars of light were shining out from the earth in all directions, effectively establishing the earth as the center of an illuminated universe. I think consciousness would continue to expand beyond that, in ways that we can't even begin to imagine at this stage of the game.

NOTE: Becoming a "pillar of light" may sound threatening to our individual identities because the ego wants to survive at all costs. That's its job in ensuring our survival and facilitating the human experience. But what if each pillar of light projected its own universe of creation, with beings and experiences so grand as to be beyond anything we can presently conceive?

Q14: What are your hopes for "The Gospel of One"?

A14: As I said, I am not an evangelist. I do not need people to agree with me, and I have no interest in being the spiritual flavor of the month, the week, or even the next fifteen minutes as far as that goes. If someone has different beliefs that give them comfort—and hopefully those beliefs are not used to attack others—then more power to them.

I think our tendency as human beings is for some "leader" to tell us what to do and to show us the way. If readers find some inspiration here, then I encourage them to use it to further their own spiritual evolution. Ultimately, the "guru" they seek is the person they see in the mirror each morning. As it says in Essay 2, "To find God, stop looking. Stop looking, and start Being."

Overall, my hope is that "The Gospel of One" provides

inspiration and a different point of view for those who are dissatisfied with what they've been taught and what they see going on in the world. My hope is that in some sense it contributes to the evolution of individual and collective consciousness, and that the world is a better place with "The Gospel of One" in it.

Q15: Any last words?

A15: I do not pretend to have all the answers, or to always live up to the high ideas with which I have become acquainted, and for myself, it seems I shall ever remain a work in progress. And that's okay. That's the ride.

Lastly, there is a saying in twelve step support groups, "Take what you like, and leave the rest." That is what I encourage readers to do here.

ABOUT THE AUTHOR

Mark Burke is the pen name of retired Information Technology manager, technical writer, photographer, digital artist, Reiki Master, holistic health advocate, spiritual explorer, and "accidental theologian" Robert Burke.

Why the use of the *nom de plume*? It's a nickname from childhood from whence these explorations originated, and therefore simply felt correct for the material.

For additional information about the author, please reference the Preface and the "Questions for the Author" section of the Addendums.

And hey, you have a lovely day out there!